HE WHO
THINKS
HAS TO
BELIEVE

HE WHO THINKS HAS TO BELIEVE

Dr. A.E. Wilder-Smith

TWFT PUBLISHERS
COSTA MESA, CALIFORNIA

He Who Thinks Has To Believe

Translated from the original German by
Petra Wilder-Smith

© 1981 A.E. Wilder-Smith

Published in collaboration with
Pro Universitate e.v. Roggern,
CH-3646, Einigen am Thunersee, Switzerland

TWFT PUBLISHERS
Box 8000
Costa Mesa, California 92628

ISBN 0-936728-30-2

Previously published by CLP, San Diego, Ca.
1981, ISBN 0-89051-073-3.
Republished by TWFT Publishers, 1988

Cataloging in Publication Data
Wilder-Smith, A. E.
　He Who Thinks Has To Believe
　by A.E. Wilder-Smith.

　1. Reasoning.　2. Evolution.　I. Title.
160

Contents

Chapter 1

Thoughts and Beliefs of The Neanderthalers

New Neanderthal Find on the Island of Papua

A Neanderthaler, living in a small tribe isolated from present-day civilization in the forests of Papua, knew nothing of modern man and modern civilization. Our technological way of life with its radios, television, telephones, and automobiles was unknown to him. He did not even know what a machine was. He lived in a pure stone age culture. Yet his thoughts were by no means primitive, for his knowledge of botany and the healing powers of various plants was extensive. Thus although he knew nothing of airplanes, his knowledge of pharmacognosy — of the heal-

ing powers of plants — was far greater than
ours. He was also quite well educated in
certain aspects of art, for he had visited some
of the caves higher up in the forests. There he
had learned how Cro-Magnon man painted
beautiful scenes on the walls of these dark
caves. With simple colors he quite artistically
portrayed animals and plants. He had also
mastered the art of drawing on bones. He
really loved all aspects of nature and knew
how to treat its plants and animals. This
small Neanderthal tribe lived together peacefully and happily in complete isolation.

One fine day our Neanderthaler leader
saw something in the sky that terrified him.
He had no idea what it could be and therefore
was very frightened. We, in his place, would
have recognized the sound of a low flying
jumbo jet, which was approaching him at
great speed and low altitude. The machine
left a long trail of black smoke in its wake
which was preceded by a long dark red burst
of flame. The jumbo jet was rapidly losing
altitude despite its increasing speed and er-
ratic flight course; it seemed to be aiming
directly for him, so the Neanderthaler hastily
fled into a nearby cave far below the earth's
surface.

Shortly afterwards there was a terrible ear shattering noise close by: trees were flattened, metal and wood crashed to the ground. Then suddenly it was uncannily quiet. Only the faint hiss and crackle of a small forest fire could be heard. The Neanderthaler waited for a few minutes, then very cautiously he crept forth from his hiding place and fearfully surveyed his surroundings. He perceived the burning remains of the huge machine that had crashed. As it crashed, the machine had exploded and razed many trees before coming to a halt. Its cargo lay scattered everywhere. Crates had been broken open by the impact of the crash. The wreck was surrounded by radios, television sets, telephones, and car engines. The half-burned remains of the crew were a hideous sight. The partly charred and terribly disfigured corpses were almost unrecognizable, although our Neanderthaler recognized them immediately as corpses of his own kind. They were, of course, the remains of modern men, homines sapientes sapientes.

With great caution he approached this terrible scene. Several small fires flickered feebly before dying out completely. Everything became very quiet — the corpses lay silent in all sorts of possible and impossible positions around the wreck. Obviously all the

passengers were dead. Frightened and deeply
shocked, our Neanderthaler surveyed the
scene of this catastrophe. Naturally he felt
helpless. What could a helpless, even though
intelligent, Neanderthaler do in this situation? Being a sensible Neanderthaler, he first
fetched his wife, who sent the children away
and forbade them to follow her. Then Mr. and
Mrs. Neanderthaler ran to the wreck with all
its terrible secrets. Having respectfully exam-
ined it all, they fetched their children to the
wreck. Having prepared them appropriately,
they shared with them this mysterious, terrible incident.

The children, once they had recovered a
little from the shock of seeing this catastrophe, began to examine the "Jumbo's" scattered cargo. Crates, some burst open, were
scattered everywhere — typewriters (it was
an export shipment), radios, TV's, and spare
parts were to be found in vast amounts in the
proximity of the wreck. The function of these
machines puzzled the Neanderthalers. In a
large, almost undamaged crate the children
found a Japanese jeep, which was even in
good working order. Inside the jeep lay all the
necessary tools for the repair and mainte-
nance of the vehicle. Just like our children,
Neanderthal children were inquisitive, as
well as quick. Once they had overcome their

initial fears, the children's curiosity prevailed.

What the Neanderthalers Learned

Very quickly the Neanderthal children had discovered how to remove and replace the jeep's wheels. The functions of the various controls were also quickly established. To their great delight, they found that turning a certain key would start up the engine. Pressing a certain pedal increased the engine speed — which could be decreased again by removing the foot from the pedal. On engaging a certain lever, simultaneously depressing another pedal, and then slowly releasing it, the jeep began to move so that it could be driven around. Their parents were initially a little frightened, but soon became braver once they had recognized the harmlessness of this machine. Soon the Neanderthal fathers and mothers with their children were riding around in the jeep. The parents also quickly learned how to drive. Once when the jeep would no longer start up, they discovered the meaning of gasoline as a fuel — gasoline cans lay scattered around the crashed jet. The exact function of gasoline as a fuel was also soon determined. After examining the cylin-

der head, the pistons, and the spark plugs,
they discovered that gasoline is burned in the
cylinder head, exerts pressure on the pistons,
and forces them downward. This movement
was then transmitted via the crank shaft and
the gears to the wheels, so that the jeep finally
moved due to the burned fuel.

Thus our Neanderthal children learned
about car driving and mechanics very quickly,
perhaps even quicker than the Pygmy children in Central Africa who learned to drive a
car within a few days, without even having
seen a car or any other machine before. Thus
we are not expecting too much of our Neanderthal children.

However, the Neanderthalers were not
only good botanists and naturalists, they
were also thinkers. They wondered about the
origin of the airplane, the machines, and the
people who had died in the plane. What was
the meaning of all these machines? Where did
they come from? It was obvious to them that
the jeep was suited to transport on the ground
and the airplane to transport in the air. The
hieroglyphics on the typewriter keys and the
numbers on the jeep's cylinder head posed a
bit of a problem. They assumed that people
similar to those who had flown in the machine
and thus died were certainly involved in the

design and the construction of the airplane and its freight.

How The Neanderthalers
Bury Their Dead

While thinking these matters over, they were faced with a problem which needed a rapid solution: what should they do with the corpses of the air crew? Decomposition had already begun. If the crew had been Neanderthalers, they could easily have coped. They would have sent the corpses and various remains on their long journey into the other world with due and respectful preparations and a solemn religious funeral, for no Neanderthaler doubted that he was made by a Creator, and that after his death he would return to this Creator in his transcendent world. This philosophy of life and of life and death seemed to them to be compellingly logical, for their train of thought ran like this: Just as a stone knife requires a maker, so a human body, which is more improbable than a stone knife and therefore will not develop spontaneously, also requires a creator. It was also clear to them that this Creator of the body does not live within time and space. For this reason, he lives in a transcendent world to which we all return at death. This was their clear and transparent philosophy of life and death.

The Neanderthaler also knew that after death his body would return to the clay of the earth. For this reason, he logically assumed that his body was built from the clay of the earth, as stone from the earth is converted into stone knives. Stone knives were made out of stone by the skill of a Neanderthaler — hard stones do not spontaneously organize themselves into stone knives. For this reason it seemed logical that clay was incorporated into Neanderthalers and animal bodies by a skilled hand, for clay did not spontaneously organize itself to form people and animals, anymore than stones spontaneously formed knives. Therefore they reasoned that a skilled being must have *worked* the clay — like the stone.

It was the Neanderthaler's life-long desire to enter into direct communication with this skilled Being. He suspected that at death this confrontation with the clay-organizer would take place. His thoughts resulted from the simple, irrefutable observations that inorganic stones do not develop into stone knives without any external help — any more than inorganic clay could produce human, animal, and plant forms. His yearning for a meeting with his primeval clay-organizer was increased by the persistent rumor that in the dim past some Neanderthalers had seen Him and even spoken with Him. These meetings were spoken of with great respect and fascination, although our Neanderthalers had little personal experience in this area.

Thus the big question for the Neanderthals was this: "Do these modern people, the victims of this airplane disaster, return to the same Creator as the Neanderthalers?" Could they be buried in the same way as Neanderthalers? After long consultations between the wise men of the tribe, the Neanderthalers buried the modern Homines sapientes sapientes just as they buried their own dead. Thus they were dispatched most honorably into the next world.

Chapter 2

The Neanderthalers as Rational Persons

A Further Big Surprise for the Neanderthalers

Just as the Neanderthalers were about to bring the funeral to an end, they heard a strange noise in the jungle below their settlement. It sounded like a group of people hacking their way through the dense jungle. Occasionally shots could be heard — a novel sound to the Neanderthalers. They hesitated a little, then continued to lay the disfigured corpses, flowers, and burnt offerings in the expressly prepared coffins. The hacking noise became louder and louder and just as the Neanderthalers were lowering the last coffin into the grave, a group of Homines sapientes reached the Neanderthal settlement.

Both groups — Neanderthalers and Homines sapientes sapientes — stared in surprise, the Neanderthalers in their festive fur clothes (for the funeral) and the modern men, sweaty and tattered after their grueling journey through the jungle. After the first embarrassed salutations — for they could hardly communicate as their languages differed quite significantly — the modern men inspected the crashed airplane, for they had been sent from afar to search for the wreck.

After the modern men had discovered that all the air crew were dead and that the Neanderthalers were about to bury them respectfully, they realized that they need not fear the "natives" — that they were "civilized." Although their dress looked "different," their behavior toward the dead proved their trustworthiness.

The Neanderthalers were somewhat more solidly built, their eyebrows bushier and more prominent, their muscles a little stronger than those of the modern men. They looked capable of throwing their spears well. Their heads, too, were a little larger than those of the modern men and their bodies stockier. But both their intelligence and mighty bodily strength were visible. Comparison is often difficult, but the Neanderthalers looked a little like the famous picture of Joseph, fettered in prison, discussing dreams with Pharaoh's baker and butler. The modern men (homines sapientes sapientes) looked more like Pharaoh's two servants, who were conversing with Joseph.

The Neanderthalers showed great friendliness toward the new arrivals; they considered all men their friends until proven otherwise. The modern men were surprised by this friendliness, for they always acted on the customary modern principle that every man is an enemy until proven to be a friend: quite a different, but widespread approach among modern, "civilized" men! Now, how were the two groups to communicate, for they shared no common language? Luckily most "primitive" men are adept at dealing with communication problems. After the Neanderthalers had left the spoil from the airplane to the modern men (they were not particularly attached to such treasures and thought that the cargo rightfully belonged to the modern men, anyway), the new arrivals inquired into the purpose of the funeral ceremonies which they had observed. Why the rites, the flowers, and the offerings? Why did they respect the decaying dead?

The Neanderthaler's Beliefs

By means of sign language, the leading Neanderthalers told the modern men that nearly all Neanderthalers believed in a transcendent, but omnipresent, omnipotent Creator of man, of the world and biology. The human body, like all animals or plants, was, after all, built from good clay, for once the body died it did revert to clay. Someone must, therefore, have shaped the clay into living human bodies, also into animals and plants, for clay could never organize itself into bodies, any more than stone would spontaneously shape itself into a stone knife. The metallic airplane components — just like stone and clay — would certainly not have produced themselves to form an airplane, thus there must have been an external creator involved. Now if it is a fact that inorganic stone does not spontaneously convert itself into stone knives, and if one accepts that inorganic non-living clay never spontaneously produces living bodies, then someone must have modeled man as he is, even modern man, too, from clay. This someone must have modeled the clay just like a Neanderthaler works on stones to produce stone knives. Stones do not spontaneously turn into stone knives.

The modern men whispered and looked amused during the Neanderthaler's discourse, which displeased the polite Neanderthaler. Finally the Neanderthaler asked what the problem was, to which the modern man replied that the Neanderthaler's statement was incorrect. For salt, when it crystallizes out of water, quite spontaneously forms salt crystals. Water, when it freezes, quite spontaneously forms ice crystals. Snow falling from the sky consists of very beautiful spontaneous crystal forms. All the Neanderthalers immediately pointed out that salt crystals and snow were not alive. The modern men insisted that life is nothing but a complex crystal. Then the conversation came to a halt. Communication problems were still too extensive to permit any further useful discussion.

Why the Neanderthalers Believe

After several weeks had passed, the two groups of men began to communicate better. Less sign language was used; the Neanderthalers began to understand and also to speak the language of the Homines sapientes sapientes. The metaphysical unbelief of the latter very much disturbed the Neanderthal-

ers, for together with the loss of their belief in
the metaphysical, they had obviously also lost
their faith in one another. The modern people
showed no respect toward the dead and very
little even for the living. This attitude very
rapidly affected their sexual habits. For the
modern men everything was free — including
the attractive, intelligent Neanderthal girls.
The Neanderthalers reacted very violently
and sourly to the seduction of their girls by the
modern men. They probably, correctly, attributed the loose morals of the modern people to
their lack of respect for the metaphysical
world.

One day, after both groups had begun to
communicate quite well, the Neanderthal
chief asked the leader of the modern men
whether his unbelief toward the Creator was
emotionally or rationally justified. Firmly the
modern man replied that all philosophical
and scientific convictions of most modern men
were based on pure reason. Rationality is the
key characteristic of modern man, he said,
visibly taken aback by the Neanderthaler's
question. But the latter continued thoughtfully and persistently to imply that the unbelief of the modern men had a purely emotional
and totally irrational basis, for during their
meals he had observed it to be a fact that the
modern men's beliefs were based on emotions

and not on rationality. Immediately the modern men took up the argument. They leaned forward to enable them to observe better around the camp fire what "revelations" the Neanderthalers were about to make, for in philosophical discussions the Neanderthalers were always highly original — their thoughts were often not only original but also most ingenious.

"Yes," continued the Neanderthaler, "in the course of our mutual socializing over the past weeks, we often sat peacefully and happily at the same table with you. We prepared for you our best dishes and likewise you also shared your best food with us. So at table our great friendship grew. Naturally we had to obtain our food fresh from the jungle. You, however, are far superior to us in some respects, for we ate from your cans and bottles. Your food, although not really fresh, tastes excellent, although we prefer truly fresh foods. Your food — sardines, ham, lentils, corn, pineapple, sausages — keeps for an unlimited time in your cans and bottles. It seems miraculous to us, for once the bottle or can has been opened, the food decays just as quickly as ours does. Furthermore, when they decay they become clay again, just as our own bodies revert to clay after death. You have told us that most modern people eat such food-

stuffs which are often several years old, yet
still taste quite fresh. Yes, you said that you
modern people have been eating preserved
food for more than one hundred years and
that you have produced billions of such cans
and bottles. Let us keep these facts in mind
while we continue our line of argument. Is
everything clear so far?"

The Neanderthalers Become Acquainted With the Conserved Foods Industries

"In our scientific discussions you have
tried to convince us that our Neanderthal
postulate on the need for a Creator to convert
the earth's clay into our bodies and those of
animals and plants is superfluous and purely
emotional. You tell us modern men have
proved that clay (matter) together with time
periods plus energy (the warmth from the
sun) suffice to ensure that clay will spontaneously organize itself into life without the aid of
any Creator outside of matter. For this reason, you say, the construction of a body from
clay in no way proves a Creator, but only that
solar energy has acted during time upon matter (clay). You have said in your language that
an open physical system will and must eventually produce life, even people ... and all this

without a Creator, without Metaphysics or additional intelligence, with neither plan nor teleonomy. Is that correct?"

"Yes," replied the modern men — obviously the Neanderthalers had absorbed well their lessons on evolution and biochemistry! "We are surprised that the Neanderthalers comprehend these issues so quickly and thoroughly. But what is the connection between all this and rational or emotional thoughts, and how is this connected with belief in a Creator?"

A few moments later, after some careful thought, our Neanderthaler continued to say that he could not bring the principle of bottled and canned food into agreement with the modern theories on the origin of life. The two just could not be brought to the same common denominator — sardine cans which keep almost indefinitely and the postulate of the spontaneous development of life within open physical systems.

The modern men gazed at each other with amazement, for they could not see any problems there. What was the connection? What were the Neanderthalers driving at? However, they knew the Neanderthalers well enough to expect real connections as seen by the wise Neanderthaler.

He continued, "You explained to us in our
science lessons that, with time, energy plus
matter (clay) spontaneously produces life,
and that this life then spontaneously develops upward by mutation and natural selection, probably via a small diversion — namely
us, the Neanderthalers — to form modern
man. Is that so?" Somewhat ashamed by this
gentle backhand, the modern men agreed.
"Now," the Neanderthaler continued, "you
yourselves claim to have manufactured billions of sardine cans and preserved meats.
Probably you have done so constantly in large
amounts over more than 100 years." "Yes,"
replied the modern men, "this is indeed so, but
please could we hurry up and get to the point."
Like any good Neanderthaler, however, their
chief tended to think slowly, thoroughly, and
very precisely.

Thoughtfully the Neanderthaler stroked
his long golden beard and said, "Did it ever
occur to you in those one hundred years, that
the canned foods industry provides you with
final proof that our postulated need for a
Creator is justified and rational, and that it is
the downfall of all your materialistic and
atheistic theories in this area?" "No!" cried the
modern men, who had congregated around
the camp fire to listen more closely, "We do not
know what you Neanderthalers are getting

at. Hurry up, we want to know." "Yes, I know that," said the wise Neanderthaler, "but first you must get back to the basics and then draw your conclusions. Naturally, the modern men were not interested in moralizing of this sort. "Well," said the Neanderthaler, "your theories state that matter (clay) plus energy plus time produces chemical evolution up to a primitive cell or a coacervate or microsphere, don't they? An open system, when it receives energy from an external source, will produce life spontaneously, with neither intelligence nor Creator to help ... this is the irrational part of your postulate." The modern men had long since lost patience with the Neanderthaler and wanted to finally cut him off. But he raised his hand and said quite determinedly, "Every sardine can and every glass of conserved meat must be considered *as an open system so far as its energetics are concerned.* The can allows heat to enter and to escape again. The can's contents can be heated or cooled at will, can it not? Therefore the system is thermodynamically completely open. Bottled meat represents an even more open system — if that is possible — for both heat and also light can easily penetrate its walls. In their energetics, both cans and glasses are widely open, thermodynamic systems. *Such systems are sealed against living spores.* Thermodynamically and energetically they are open. It should not matter that they are closed to living spores, for according to your theories such spores should develop easily in any place where only matter, time and energy are present. Matter and energy are plentifully available in all cans and glasses. The simple shutting out of spores in cans should not be relevant from your viewpoint. According to you, only energy, time and matter are important, and these are plentiful in each can and every glass. For this reason all sorts of simple spores should have developed long ago, for you have repeated the experiment billions of times, and this under the most favorable experimental conditions for archebiopoesis. In experimental reality," added the Neanderthaler, "the shutting out of spores has proved far more important than the provision of energy. According to your theories the provision of energy should be the most important factor involved in archebiopoesis in a can; but this is obviously not the case."

"How often," inquired the wise Neanderthaler, "during one hundred years of producing billions of units of canned and preserved foods, have you observed that energy in an energetically open system — such as a sardine can — plus sardine corpses (ideal material for building bodies and cells — far more so than a hypothetical primeval soup) produces new forms of — even very primitive — life? *Never,* by your own words. Billions of sardine experiments have shown without a doubt that energy plus matter (sardines) plus time have never produced life, not even under the most favorable conditions. This fact is so certain and so well proved that an entire industry — the canning industry — depends on it. If this fact were not so definite and life did after all develop in these cans from time to time, then your canned foods industry would be *totally* useless. Why, then, do you claim the opposite to be results of this experiment, just to support your materialistic theories and postulates? We say that matter plus energy plus know-how (from a Creator or from a programmed genetic code [spore] devised by a Creator) results in life. You, however, claim that matter plus energy plus time alone gives life, and that we, therefore, require neither a Creator nor his program (spore) to conceive life. We have experimental evidence behind our faith and are therefore *rational.* You cannot produce a single experiment to confirm your materialistic claims! For this reason you are, as we have already repeatedly said, purely emotional, yes, even schizophrenic — i.e., separated from experimental reality—in your beliefs. How can you aspire to being

experimental scientists, if you do not take the
slightest notice of billions of experiments
from your own industries? Experimental evidence, and therefore rationality, stand fully
behind our Neanderthaler belief in a Creator.
We are rational beings. You are stubborn and
purely emotional and also schizophrenic in
your materialism and atheism. This experiment also leaves you inexcusable, i.e. *without
any excuse* — for your atheism and materialism."

"But let us not forget the other side of the
picture. How often have you confirmed that
life's spores plus matter and energy produce
life (depending on the sort of spore)? Every
time any of life's spores, i.e. programs, penetrate a sardine can, new life results, does it
not? From this fact we Neanderthalers con-
clude that dead matter (clay or sardine
corpses) plus energy plus life's *programs* produce life and that just these programs are not
present in inorganic matter. Your theories
require that at least occasionally in the course
of billions of experiments life develop from
clay (inorganic matter) and energy. Unfortu-
nately for you and your theories this has
never happened experimentally, despite billions of experiments."

The old Neanderthaler concluded his discourse with the following words: 'Your unbelief in a Creator (atheism and materialism) is in no way linked to being educated in scientific experimental matters. All scientific proofs are available and all demonstrate that life only stems from life or *life programs*. All programs, however, finally originate from *intelligent beings, without exception*. Even if a computer can program itself, it initially required preprogramming by a human being to develop these programs. Now, as one or more persons are at the root of any program and as life consists of various genetic and other programs, we Neanderthalers believe in a Programmer or Creator who originally programmed us — and you, too."

"We also believe that a living Creator made us or our seed and our programs. To claim that a program programmed itself from nothing is *emotional, schizophrenic, and non-rational*. We Neanderthalers have learned much from you modern men — e.g. how to program certain computers. But we have also learned that only living persons devise and create programs. If we can read and decipher and program, we know that we can think in the same manner as the programmer himself. As you modern men can read the program within our own genetics, we assume that we humans can to a minor extent think as our Creator thought originally in order to program us. Thus the programmed beings learn to understand the Programmer. We assume, therefore, that we are able to think a little as our Creator thinks. We are made in His image, therefore." The Neanderthaler closed with the impressive words: "Did not one of your thinkers say: 'We are the offspring of God!' Therefore we are the same species as God himself, although we are fallen Gods (Acts 17:28, 29)." The Neanderthalers had somehow discovered one of the modern men's Bibles and had read it with much zeal!

In the following partly heated conversation, the Neanderthalers showed quite clearly their conviction that the modern men suffered more from lack of *will* than from lack of *ability* to believe. A young Neanderthaler added that the modern men did not believe because they preferred to live without belief. "Your unbelief and your atheism have no experimental/rational basis, they are purely emotion," said the Neanderthalers. "In reality they are nothing but a rebellion against your own rationale and common sense. For this reason your world is, as you have told us, filled with violent rebellion, war, murder, and destruction. You rebel against yourselves and gently need to rethink, otherwise you will destroy yourselves — and us."

Thus ended their evening together, Silently each group went its own way.

Chapter 3

The Neanderthalers Think Rationally

The Further Development Of The Neanderthaler's Argument

At first the modern men were very quiet and also a little stunned by the "uncivilized" Neanderthalers' arguments. But after a few days the two groups were on just as good terms again. One week later the modern men invited the Neanderthalers again to a joint meal to continue the previous conversation. All sorts of exotic dishes were presented — mostly in their conserved form, of course — for the modern men had brought all sorts of things with them.

Once the meal was over (even wine, Coca
Cola, and fruit juices had been served), the
modern men's spokesman said that the
Neanderthaler's line of argument was completely wrong. It must be wrong, otherwise all
modern humanity would be mistaken, for
modern men today can, with no trouble, develop new life from sardine proteins in a tin
can, and this without adding life spores or
God's assistance! A certain scientist by the
name of Sol Spiegelman had taken apart an
organism (virus) and had even crystallized
the dead components (the program for primitive life can be crystallized); he then put them
back together again under sterile (germ-free)
conditions and finally incorporated them into
a new host organism. No living spore was
added, but Spiegelman's virus — constructed
from *dead* components — *lived,* for it under-
went replication. Thus, life occurs spontaneously after all, without adding living genetic
information from dead preserved matter. "If
this can be done once in the laboratory, it
might also have happened at the beginning of
all life! So you Neanderthalers are upholding
your argument with incorrect facts. The modern men's argument proves irrefutably the
fact that no metaphysical God is needed to
make life. Inorganic, dead chemistry is, after
all, responsible for life."

At this moment the Neanderthalers appeared to be overcome by a violent fit. Even the chief Neanderthal spokesman did not seem momentarily capable of speech. Some immature modern men, having observed that this violent fit was affecting all the Neanderthalers simultaneously, decided that it must be a fit of laughter. Others attributed it to the effects of Coca Cola on the Neanderthalers who weren't used to it. In any case, the fit soon subsided and the conversation could be continued.

The polite Neanderthaler apologized for their fit and began immediately. Their spokesman pointed out that according to the modern men's teachings it is the genetic information that produces life from the dead sardine proteins and introduces the genetic ideas into the code of the DNA molecule of its particular type (viruses, bacteria, frogs, birds, or mammals). These ideas, projects, and concepts are written on the DNA molecule in its genetic language. They are the chemical instructions required to produce life from dead proteins. "Is this not true?" The modern men agreed unanimously. "Genetics," continued the Neanderthaler, "contain the chemical instructions necessary to produce living molecules from dead ones. It could be said that genetics are a recipe book for the

project of life, set in a language that we can
even partly read today." The modern men
confirmed the veracity of the Neanderthaler's statement.

Genetic Ideas

"Good," said the Neanderthaler, "then
we need only take one more step to show that
your modern arguments are unacceptable.
Normally new life develops *from the ideas*
which are written on zygotes in their genetic
chemical language. Now your Sol Spiegelman
read and understood these genetically stored
ideas and transformed them into chemical
reactions. Normally the genetic ideas come
directly from the genetic information into the
dead proteins where they organize the proteins into life. Now Sol Spiegelman injected
the same genetic ideas *directly* into the dead
chemical molecules, so that these same ideas
brought the proteins to life. This proves what
the Neanderthalers have always believed,
that there is only one formula for life:"

matter plus energy plus ideas plus time = life

"It is all the same whether these ideas are stored in the chemistry of genetics or in Sol Spiegelman's head. The application of the ideas provides the same result — life. But without them, there is no life."

"Different ideas produce different types of life. But matter and energy without ideas give no life at all. Surely the sealed sardine cans prove this — the *ideas* of life (genetic projects, spores) do not penetrate into the sealed cans."

"But if ideas or concepts (logos) in the form of genetic information or the technical know-how of a Sol Spiegelman (again Logos/Telos) penetrate into our otherwise sealed sardine cans, they will 'explode' with life. The ideas can even be stored in genetic language on a crystallized virus as long as a host organism is somehow present providing metabolic energy. The matter of the sardine corpses is only 'waiting' for such concepts or ideas (logos, spirit, telos), and then it will burst into life. But without the ideas of logos or telos, not one single can of the billions produced in the entire history of the more than hundred-year-old conserved foods industry has awakened to any form of life. Provide logos, spirit, idea, or code — concept ('breath' or whatever) and life will spring from dead matter, just as described in Genesis. But without Ideas, Spirit, Breath, or Logos, life has never awakened in

the entire history of mankind. Energy and
matter never produce even a trace of life if
'Spirit' (Idea) is not added in some form."

"For this reason we Neanderthalers believe in a Logos — a Creator of life — who took
matter and 'breathed' spirit, logos, ideas, instructions 'into' it. Depending on the logos —
ideas imposed on matter — the various sorts
were created. But ... no species without spe-
cies-ideas! We," he said, "believe in a great,
invisible Creator full of ideas or logos. *Hence*
He must be a person, *for only persons have
ideas which they then realize.* We worship this
personal Creator, who is full of ideas, as the
source of all good ideas and projects. The fact
that we have some ideas proves, does it not,
that we were created in his image (= the same
idea-filled species as God himself). For this
reason we believe that our faith in such a
creator is fully rational, and that your belief is
purely emotional. Because you only live emotionally, you live in rebellion against your own
ratio and against your own rational Creator.
You rebel against the experimental rational
facts. For this reason, you can only 'believe'
emotionally."

"Even your Greeks knew all that, for they
called this Creator 'logos' — the source of all
ideas and projects. Life is an idea, a project, a
teleonomy executed in matter. You have

turned life into a non-idea, a non-project, a non-teleonomy ... into chance. For this reason you are in a conflict with the facts of nature and are therefore without peace, rebellious, schizophrenic, and frustrated in all that you do and are."

"To claim that non-idea (= chance, stochastic molecular movements) is identical with idea, project, plan (= non-chance) is simply schizophrenic — unrelated to reality. Thus you will destroy yourselves, as well as both our world and yours."

At the end of this discussion, the young Neanderthalers discussed various possible means of solving the modern men's frustration — how it could be that Homo sapiens thinks so irrationally in the most important matters of life, i.e. in his evaluation of the meaning of life, of its origin and its destiny, despite his technical superiority to the Neanderthalers. "They are technically advanced," said the Neanderthalers, "but philosophically and logically degenerate." This was the unanimous decision reached by the young Neanderthalers. But why were the modern men so irrational in their world view? "Experimentally they are strong, but in the rational application of their experiments they are weak. Why?" Some considered the modern men to be the same species as the

Neanderthalers, but representing somewhat
degenerated Neanderthalers. Their heads,
for example, were smaller. Hence it should
follow that, together with the degeneration of
brain volume, the skeleton and muscle
strength of the modern men showed a simul-
taneous parallel degeneration. The capacity
for logical thought was certainly degenerate,
without, however, affecting his purely technical capabilities.

The Inquisitive Neanderthaler

Small groups of Neanderthalers sat
around with small groups of homines sapientes sapientes and discussed further secrets of
the human, animal, and plant body. The teen-
agers among the Neanderthalers very quickly
and gladly learned the scientific secrets of the
modern men. Additionally, they had time and
leisure, which would not have been so easily
possible under industrialized conditions. On
the average, they only needed two or three
hours a day to provide food and maintain their
homes, then they were free.

The Neanderthalers were very impressed
to discover that all the instructions and ideas
required to construct a man (from clay) are
present in a chemical language in every zy-

gote from every human sperm and every human egg. They were very surprised to discover that the language of these instructions had already been partly deciphered. For example, the chemical instructions for building insulin are already known and can, when transferred into certain bacteria, be used so that the bacterium builds human insulin, although it does not require insulin for itself. As one half of all chemical instructions are from the mother and the other half from the father, the couple's children resemble their parents or their ancestors.

Joy Among The Neanderthalers

The Neanderthalers were most surprised to learn that on every fertilized egg (zygote) chemical instructions exist for building man and all his progeny from matter (clay). These instructions, a necessity for the construction of a man, would require an entire library containing 1,000 volumes of five hundred pages each, in the smallest print, if written in English on paper. Thus each male's sperm and each female's ovum functions like a miniaturized library filled with written chemical ideas ... instructions to build men (or animals or plants) from clay. When the modern men

showed them, on paper, how the genetic instructions looked, how they read and execute
themselves (with the aid of ribosomes), how
they multiply, and also correct themselves,
the Neanderthalers were quite overcome
with joy at the Creator's grand ideas and his
incredibly miniaturized technique. They
whistled and sang improvised songs about
their great Creator when they discovered his
wisdom in gene replication. They were liter-
ally speechless, and then again filled with
wonder at the chemical miracle of cell divi-
sion. The Creator's all-surpassing intelligence and his overflowing chemical and
teleonomic ideas in the various instructions
for building various species from clay were
the topic of their evening conversation for
days, of their admiration and also of their
songs.

The modern men remained totally cool
and untouched at the Neanderthalers' mani-
festations of joy and admiration. They hardly
said a word about these wonders or about
their Neanderthal pupils' joy. For the modern
men, the writing on the genes was no proof at
all that these had either been written or
developed by a Creator. For them, the laws of
nature and properties of matter had written
and designed everything. A Creator had nothing to do with it at all. They simply considered

the Neanderthalers naive and emotional. As they attributed matter and its characteristics to purely stochastic factors, chance and the laws of nature alone were the final cause of the entire genetic code and its chemical projects. For them the entire genetic mechanism, as well as its contents, developed by chance (stochastically), for them the genetic language, with all its grammar, punctuation, correction mechanisms (necessary, should faults develop), its content of chemical ideas and projects (to build eyes, muscles, ears, livers, kidneys, hair, bones, connective tissue, hearts, lymphatics, etc.) also developed purely stochastically.

Chance was, of course, sorted out by natural selection, but natural selection itself created nothing; it only sorted out that which was supposedly provided by chance. For this reason belief in a constructive Creator of all these organs and the information and code involved therein was considered to be totally superfluous by the modern men. The nucleotides, deoxyribose, and the guanine, thymine, uracil, cytosine, and adenine molecules supposedly formed the DNA molecule (in helical form) under the influence of the laws of nature present in all matter. At the same time — or with time — the grammar and punctuation of the genetic language developed, guided by

the same laws of nature. Chance and the laws
of nature then provided plans for hearts, kidneys, brains (electronically-based computers
with millions of switching mechanisms to
provide intelligence and consciousness), for
bones, neurons (nerves), and eyes. Also for
nerve endings to equip the organism with
taste and sensation, for a cerebellum to establish equilibrium, for tongues to speak, plus a
computer to control the tongue and coordi-
nate speech, for cells producing blood and
lymph, hearts capable of pumping blood constantly over seventy years, while simultaneously undergoing repair processes, diges-
tive systems, which at a slightly elevated
temperature break down fats, carbohydrates,
and proteins into their constituents, repair
mechanisms to heal any wound — briefly, all
the know how that sets indescribably high
requirements; all this developed by itself according to modern man, by chance and from
the laws of nature.

The Skeptical Young Neanderthaler

The Neanderthalers sat very still while
these accomplishments of chance (stochastic
phenomena) and the laws of nature were
being listed. Then a young Neanderthaler,

who had remained silent so far because of his youth, arose. Timidly he inquired before the older Neanderthalers and modern men whether all these accomplishments of chance and the laws of nature would fit into the categories of projects or teleonomy. "Yes, this was certainly the case," said the modern men. "In that case," replied the young Neanderthaler, "your three laws of thermodynamics which determine all physics and chemistry must be in error, for surely the laws state that matter has neither project content nor teleonomy? So are stochastic phenomena processes that *organize* or *disorganize*? If matter is agitated, will it build a machine? Can chance plan and project a machine or devise a meaningful language, for men, animals, and plants are all biological machines built by means of a programmed language? Can chance, collaborating with the non-teleonomic machine or program? If not, then your atheistic theories are nonsensical."

The Paper Wrote The Book

The modern men remained superciliously silent. After some time the Neanderthalers' old spokesman rose again to summarize. "Really," he said, "you postulate that matter plus

stochastic phenomena wrote the genetic code
with its linguistic and instructional content."
The modern men replied stubbornly that this
was so. "Good," said the Neanderthaler, "may
I then speak more clearly?" They nodded. "In
reality," he said, "you are asking us to believe
that the paper on which the text of a book is
written has developed not only the language
in which the book is written, but also all its
concepts, ideas, and thoughts. According to
you, the paper wrote the entire book. Even its
binding and chapter headings are due to the
paper alone. However, we, the Neanderthalers, are not prepared to believe that the paper
wrote the book, including its language, ideas,
vocabulary, and chapter headings, of its own
accord. We regard such a postulate as schizophrenic — if I may speak so plainly," he said,
"far removed from reality, i.e. schizophrenic.
If the modern men believe that paper, i.e. the
matter, the clay from which we are built,
wrote our genetic 'recipe book' (the genetic
code), then your thought processes are emotional and not rational. We, the Neanderthalers, believe in an Author who wrote the book
of life — just as any other book, without
exception, was written by an *author*, and *not*
the *paper,* for life consists of various genetic
books — a different genetic book for each kind
of life. But as the genetic language, the ge-

netic code, is identical in all forms of life (only the content varies, according to the sort of life), we believe in a *single personal Author,* who always employed the same language to store and realize all his ideas, projects, and life concepts. We regard our belief in a Creator as rational, as experimentally justifiable, far more rational than your rebellion against your own ratio (common sense), and against recognizing the author of the genetic book of life. You must revise your thoughts immediately or you will die of emotionally-conditioned schizophrenia, totally removed from reality.[1] You are excellent technicians, but no thinkers."

The young Neanderthalers unanimously confirmed this conviction. Some of the modern men thought these arguments through; a few even revised their opinions before they broke up to return to their world. Before they left, amid many demonstrations of affection and friendship, the Neanderthalers obtained their promise not to divulge their presence in

----

[1]The results of the latest medical research into schizophrenia, *cf* "A Singular Solution for Schizophrenia ," David Horrobin, *New Scientist,* February 28, 1980, Vol. 85, No. 1196, p. 642-644. Horrobin holds the opinion that schizophrenia may, among other factors, be linked with defects in prostaglandin-E-l metabolism.

the high altitude jungles of Papua to the rest
of the world. Although the Neanderthalers
had come to appreciate the modern cans and
machines, they preferred living primitively in
a rational world of belief to spending their
days in the midst of material plenty, but
schizophrenically in an emotional, rebellious
world of unbelief.

Ilya Prigogine and Archebiopoesis

At this stage it must be added that in 1979
Prigogine won the Nobel prize for his work on
the spontaneous structuring of systems in a
state of non-equilibrium.[2] This was used
throughout the world by materialists (and
also by Prigogine) to prove the possibility of
spontaneous biogenesis from unstructured
matter. In this manner the impossibility, according to the second law of thermodynamics,
of spontaneous structuring upward to finally
result in life, was thought to have been
avoided.

---

[2] *cf* P, Glansdorff, I. Prigogine, "Thermodynamic Theory
of Structure, Stability, and Fluctuations, *Wiley
Interscience,* John Wiley & Sons Ltd., London, New
York, Sydney, & Toronto, reprinted 1978.

This somewhat premature conclusion regarding the possibility of a spontaneous structuring of matter into life (biogenesis) reached by the materialists must be considered, keeping in mind that Prigogine only investigated systems well out of equilibrium. Such systems are, therefore, irreversible and have nothing in common with the organic-chemical systems of reactions which might possibly be involved in biogenesis. Such organic-chemical systems, which supposedly spontaneously provided the original building materials of life, are, of course, as every organic chemist knows, strictly reversible (apart from certain known "entropy holes"), so that Prigogine's otherwise so important work is totally irrelevant here.

Chapter 4

Creation or Chance?

A Creator—But of What Sort?

Thought processes should lead to every conviction, i.e. to every belief—or also to every unbelief—unless emotions overshadow or eliminate those "thought processes." The convinced atheist — believing that there is no God — as well as the theist, who by means of deliberations and thought processes has come to the conclusion that a Creator does exist — each should reach his conviction by thought processes rather than by mere emotional sway.

It is impossible to force oneself to a belief in anything. If we try to force ourselves into any belief without thought processes, the result is a hysteria, which differs vastly from a true conviction or a genuine belief. If any sect were to require of its followers the "belief" that Jonah swallowed the whale, then they could certainly force themselves to do so purely emotionally, in order to "believe" such a dogma. However, the "belief" in this dogma would be purely emotionally based hysteria and would have little connection with any really rational conviction. Thus many people try to "believe" emotionally in the dogmas of a religion which are, however, often as nonsensical and irrational as the dogma that "Jonah swallowed the whale." It is just for this reason that many churches and congregations suffer from dangerous emotionalism and hysteria. Ratio —i.e., a good *reason* for rationally accepting a dogma—would lead to genuine conviction and thus also to a powerful faith, for man is rightly called Homo sapiens—he is not satisfied until convinced rationally. Only after a man is *convinced* and *acts accordingly,* is he justifiably flooded by emotions such as love, joy, and peace—*after* satisfying his ratio. If however, he does not obey and use his ratio, he is overcome by negative emotions— hysteria, frustration, disappointment, and unhappiness.

Thus belief is a sort of rational conviction—a certain faith in rational, even though often invisible, hopes. However, it cannot be forced without thought processes. A rational basis for the conviction must exist—even if the basis of this conviction is the existence of an omnipotent, omniscient God.

The Four Pillars of Faith

Now which kind of conviction (belief, faith) regarding the existence of an almighty God can we hold rationally? Four different beliefs exist.

1. There is no Creator God. Matter was and is eternal and therefore requires no Creator to make it and the life springing from it. This belief is called atheism.
2. There is an almighty Creator, who may be personal or not, who created and maintains the world. This belief is called theism.
3. There is an almighty Creator who in the beginning created the world and biology. He may be personal or not. But since time he created and "wound up" everything, he no longer involves himself with his creation anymore, he simply allows it all to "run down." This belief is called deism and is often linked with the "God is dead" theology.

4. An almighty Creator exists, who is, however, identical with the cosmos and the matter of the universe. All men and all molecules of the universe are a part of this omnipresent Creator. The Hindus believe this. For this reason they think that they and all animals are parts and various aspects of God. This conviction is called pantheism. The God of the pantheists is usually taken impersonally.

In the previous chapters we have seen that it is difficult to defend the atheistic solution of the God-dilemma truly rationally. The evidence of the properties of matter demonstrates it is not creative. So how can creation be explained without a Creator if matter itself is not creative?

In considering this question it must be remembered that the properties of matter and energy must have been constant from the beginning; otherwise primitive carbon would not have been carbon in the modern sense of the word. Now if matter and energy today are not creative, then accordingly they were not creative in the beginning either, for their properties have *by definition* remained constant. Under these conditions we must ask ourselves why in the beginning life supposedly developed from matter and energy spontaneously, but today it does not. The only

squarely rational reply to this question is, of
course, that at biogenesis an environment
different from that known to us today acted on
primitive nature. But in principle, from the
point of our time-space continuum, our material and environment has remained the same.
Why did "spontaneous" biogenesis take place
then, and not today?

We are compelled to suggest a different
type of environment, an environment of ideas
which in those days acted upon the matter
(which in itself was "idea-less") and which no
longer acts in nature today, for matter, then as
now, is itself without ideas. For this reason it
needs, now as it did then, to be acted upon by
ideas in order to bring about biogenesis. Now
we are on the right track, for *the ideas* of a
biochemist do bring matter to life today—as
they did in the beginning. Experimental evidence from the laboratory proves this fact
over and over again. Providing matter with a
"rational" environment, i.e. one of logos or
telos, produces life today—as it did in the
beginning. Only thus can the fact be explained that matter with constant non–creative properties does and did carry, again and
again, the concepts of life.

Logos—mind—acts on matter and energy
now as it did then, to produce the ideas and
concepts of life. At this stage of insight it is

simply no longer possible to remain either an
atheist or a materialist. The facts simply
preclude both of these philosophies. So, at this
stage, we will not enter into belief No. 1
(atheism) any further. But how are we to cope
with the three other possibilities, theism,
deism, and pantheism? How are we to form an
opinion here?

Both deism and theism can presuppose a
personal or an impersonal God. Pantheism
normally requires an impersonal God, for
there God is nature and nature is God. If the
term nature is taken only to include matter
and energy, then obviously this God cannot be
personal, for the universe of inorganic matter
is obviously not "personal" in the usual sense
of the word. Raw matter is neither intelligent
nor does it possess consciousness, as far as we
know; therefore it is impersonal.[1]

Once we have established that a Creator
must exist, we must pose our second question:
Is the Creator personal or not? Of course, we
cannot *imagine* or conceive an omnipresent,
eternal, or omnipotent Being—whether personal or not, for our thought apparatus is not
capable of imagining anything unlimited or

[1] cf A.E. Wilder-Smith: *Der Mensch—ein Sprechender
Computer*, Schulte-Gerth-Verlag, Asslar, Germany,

infinite. We can, e.g., only think aided by temporal limitations, one thought *after* the next, which we express by the term "time." If we speak of the term "eternity," our thought apparatus can no longer cope, for "eternity" thoroughly eliminates time—and thus a *component of our thoughts.*

Thus with even our best will we are incapable of *sensibly* contemplating the term eternity or an eternal God, for our sense (thought) is limited by time. For this reason, we do not wish to be so unreasonable as to attempt thoughts about an *eternal, omnipotent* God. We must abstain from attempts to enter into unlimited, eternal thoughts, for in this area we will produce no sense. It is just for this reason that so many religions attempting to deal with God, the eternal, contradict each other and make little sense. They must be contradictory, for "God, the Eternal, the Almighty, the Unlimited" cannot be successfully dealt with by our thought apparatus. So we shall avoid thoughts and questions of this sort which only prove "indigestible" to our minds.

Personal or Impersonal?

The question of whether or not God is personal is more easily approached by our thought apparatus. Also the question of his intelligence can be investigated by us. Intelligence is often defined as the capacity to profit from past experience. Thus, intelligence requires a memory—so that the past can be taken into account. However, an *eternal* God cannot possess a memory–in our sense of the word– because for him there are no events in the *past to consider*. Everything is in the "eternal" present! But within our time-space continuum he can have profit from a memory, otherwise he would be less than his creation, less than we are, if he possessed no memory in our dimension. As the greater creates the lesser, God must be greater than man and therefore possess—seen from within time—a longer memory and greater intelligence than man.

But is something intelligent always and automatically a person? No, for a properly programmed computer can learn to play chess better than I can and thus it will eventually beat me. So, according to our definition this machine is certainly intelligent. But is it therefore automatically a person? No, for the intelligent computer has no consciousness, i.e. no self recognition (Cogito, ergo sum).[2] Higher animals can reflect on themselves to a small degree. Certain types of apes recognize themselves in the mirror and probably reflect on themselves. Even less intelligent animals such as cows practice a pecking order—one cow is the leader and allows no other cow to go first—and hence "reflects" on its position in the herd.

We practice self-reflection and are therefore persons. However, our personality has very little to do with our intelligence. Certain people who are without doubt personalities, do not need to be very intelligent. Here again, we shall apply the same principles of thought to decide whether God is a person in this sense of the word: the greater made the lesser. If we are persons with self-reflection then accordingly God must be a greater person with greater self-reflection. By this principle he can hardly be less than a person—even a sub-person—he can hardly be less than the people he created. For this reason we assume that God must be super-person. This leads to the thought that he not only reflects on himself; he will also reflect on us—our deeds, our behavior. People reflect on other people. He

---

[2] "I think, therefore I am," Descartes

will also adapt his mode of action according to
our deeds: intelligence requires that he
should "profit" from our mode of action, as he
possesses a memory for us within time.

If God is a super–intelligent, super–personality (for his creatures, people, are after all
intelligent personalities and for this reason
the creator must surpass them in intelligence
and personality), he will also be capable of
expression—he will "speak," express his ideas
and even put them into practice. Briefly, he
must be a great logos (word)—just as man is
a lesser logos. Thus our rational thought processes would lead us to the statement that
God must be a personal logos, for if he is "only"
an intelligent *spirit* who neither speaks nor
expresses himself, then he would be less than
a person, then he would be impersonal or less
than personal.

These thoughts result from the principle
that the superior created the inferior. Man
could perhaps synthesize a virus or a bacterium, for viruses and bacteria are incompara-
bly less complex than man. But our Creator,
who must be infinitely intelligent and a super-personality to us, could never be created
by us, for as a super-personality he is far
greater than men, who are mere personalities. The Bible, of course, teaches that the
Creator is super-intelligent. Additionally he

possesses a super–consciousness, for he reflects on his super–self (the three persons of
the Trinity love each other—the Father loves
the Son and has given everything into his
hands John 3:35]). Also he is the logos and has
developed ideas and pro-jects which he expresses. As logos he wrote the ten commandments "with his own hand," as reported by
Moses.

Philosophizing and Its Limitations

In this area, however, little progress is
made by philosophizing. For this reason we
shall leave this aspect of faith as it is. Let us
now approach another very urgent question.
Can man as man "sensibly" experience such a
super–being, if such a super-personality really does exist? Surely an important pleasure
in life is meeting with other personalities,
"experiencing" them, and gaining from this
experience. Surely we are all enriched most
by meeting and experiencing again and again
true personalities during our careers. I, personally, owe very many treasures of all sorts
to contacts with other personalities. Now if a
super-intelligent, super-person who is my
Creator does exist, and if I was created in his
image (although much smaller, yet in his

image in thought-structure), then I will profit
and be enriched by any contact with him. Also
if he created us in his image and I resemble
him and he is like me as a person to a certain
extent, then he will desire fellowship with
others like us, for people are interested in one
another—if they are normal people, otherwise they are sick.

Our next question must be: Can I establish contact with the super-personality that is
my Creator? Surely it is clear that I as a
limited human being cannot comprehend
him, as he is unlimited, eternal, almighty,
omniscient, and omnipotent, which must be
strictly incomprehensible to me. So any contact on a "sensible" basis is simply impossible.
Thus, there remains only one possibility for
establishing sensible contact — the super—
creator would have to come down to our wavelength." He would have to become a man such
as we are. The only way for an animal to really
understand a man is for it to become a man. If
I had been born as a calf, I would have no
difficulty in understanding "cow" language. If
a man wishes to understand God's language
there are only two means of overcoming the
"speech barrier" between God and man: (1)
Man becomes God, or (2) God becomes man.
Only if (1) or (2) occur will God and man be on

a common wavelength, and only then will they really be able to communicate.

Contact Between Personalities

We must still ask ourselves another basic question: How is contact with another person established in the first place? How does one "experience" another person? It is very important to find the correct reply to this question, otherwise misunderstandings will arise later on.

Who and what the personality of a human (or an animal) is, no one really knows. It is not simply the thought capacity of a man, for a computer thinks (thus it possesses thought capacity)—and even thinks much more rapidly than man—yet it (the computer) is no personality. A personality reads the perceptions of its computer-brain, but is not only a computer (brain) or thought capacity. A TV faithfully reproduces pictures of the distant reality without ever being *aware* of the image on its screen. It is the person *outside the TV, sitting in front of the screen, who is aware* of the picture. Neither the brain nor the TV perceive, this is done by the ego, the personality. It is the personality which lives outside the dimension of the electronic machine (the

brain, the wiring) that is aware; just like the
person sitting in front of the TV is experiencing perception while living in a different me-
chanical dimension from that of the TV itself.
Man possesses an additional dimension to the
TV—that of his personality, which *perceives.*
The TV itself does not perceive, although it
projects the image onto the screen.

Thus man's personality lives in a dimension of its own, in a world of perception. It does
not live in the world of machines, which have
no personality and therefore cannot perceive.

This fact has an important consequence:
It is only possible to contact a personality
indirectly via its "TV apparatus," i.e. via its
five senses, through the wiring of the brain,
The person himself is separated from the
purely material world by an "event horizon."
The material world is presented to the person
under the guise of electronic pictures of reality. The person himself is "hidden," and materialistic science has not yet discovered the
secret of personality and will not discover it,
either, for materialistic science does not believe in other dimensions, realities which are
in principle inaccessible from time and matter.[3] And it is in such a dimension, concealed

---

[3]cf A.E. Wilder-Smith: *Die Demission des wissen-
schaftlichen Materialismus,* Hänssler-Verlag,
Neuhausen-Stuttgart, Germany.

from our present-day research, that human personality in God's image exists within its own dimensions.

Contact With the Creator?

Here we are brought back to our central question: How will the Creator meet us and we him? How is a dialogue established with him? How does he approach us? First we must realize that a dialogue requires two personalities—the speaker and the listener. Both must speak and both must also listen. The major question concerning the Creator and us is and remains quite practical: How?

It is impossible to argue over or discuss certain things. As C.S. Lewis once said, it is impossible to philosophize (at least with any prospect of success) whether or not the cat is in the linen cupboard. The cat can neither be seen nor heard. It is just absent. There is only one means of discovering whether the cat is in the cupboard, i.e. go to the cupboard, open the door, and look in — and there she is, purring happily.

Similarly, there is only one method of experiencing a personality, for it (the personality) is, so to speak, sitting behind its event horizon in the "cupboard" in its other dimen-

sion. We miss it and seek it. No amount of
philosophy will help here; one must "go" and
search for it where it is — in the dimension of
personality.

In a great crowd thousands of people are to
be seen. It is possible to select one person or
also a small group from the crowd and to
attempt a dialogue with him or it. If a reply is
forthcoming, the mutual experience has begun. If there is no reply, I can do nothing to
bring about a dialogue. We are here, of course,
referring to experiencing a personality by
means of a dialogue. *Now, is such an experience objective or subjective?* This is an important point! For the experience of another person is, essentially, purely *subjective and not
objective.* Thus, another personality is experienced via one's own personality, i.e. purely
*subjective*ly. It is, therefore, in the nature of a
personal encounter, of a personal experience
or of a dialogue with another personality, that
it is subjective and not objective. Thus, also, is
our experience of the super–personality
which we call the Creator. This experience
and this encounter with him must, by its
nature, be purely personal, subjective, and
confined to the individual heart, soul, or personality. It is impossible to philosophize or
argue about it objectively. Perhaps it may be
possible to see objectively that a person has

met and experienced a great personality, for such an encounter would not leave him unchanged. How much more would it be impossible for a subjective encounter with the super–personality called our Creator to leave us unaffected!

Innumerable witnesses are alive today who obviously have come out of such an encounter as totally changed people. The Bible speaks of many such changed people and refers to such a powerful experience as being born again.

These facts cannot be denied simply because they are subjective or because such a rebirth has not been experienced personally. Of course, all such encounters are subjective, and not everyone does experience such an encounter. The very nature of such an encounter with another personality requires it to be subjective. Therefore, it must always remain the subjective secret of those who have made the encounter—although they can witness to such an encounter. Why is it, then, that very many people seek such an encounter with their Creator—and do not find it?

The reason is very simple if we ask ourselves a further simple question: What hinders most the mutual subjective experience of two personalities? How is it that husband and wife can totally miss experiencing or really

encountering one another in the same house?
Although they live together, their souls are
lonely. Why do they not experience each
other's personalities? Because the one personality has often made itself "impossible"
with the other. If I am insulted, lied to,
abused, or even ignored and left to myself by
another person, I will, of course, consider this
behavior "impossible."

The opposite, of course, applies too! People
behaving thus will never find each other and
their respective personalities. People who un-
justifiably write or speak evil of me (and if I
become aware of this), will not experience me,
unless they fulfill one condition—that the
culprit, if he really values my acquaintance,
comes to me to apologize. I must, of course, act
likewise, if I am at fault, otherwise I shall
never personally experience and enjoy my
partner either.

The theologians of the past understood
this fact much better than many of their
colleagues do today, for in the past they
taught that fellowship between two persons
was harmed by infringing the laws governing
personal relationships. Speaking plainly, sin
between two persons (to use the old theologi-
cal term) separates them. Until the infringement is removed between the people and they

are thus reconciled, fellowship between the two will not be reestablished.

These facts demonstrate that in the past the nature of our personality and the laws governing personal relationships were perhaps better understood than today, for today some think that by a forced "dialogue" between two estranged people, fellowship and mutual experience are possible, even without complete reconciliation. Only a thorough reconciliation brings two estranged persons together again. But without this, no true interpersonal fellowship or experience can be reestablished. As none of us are perfect, this thorough reconciliation has to happen again and again, if interpersonal fellowship and real encounters are to be permanent and also to grow.

Could this not provide at least one explanation for the fact that many people never in their lifetime experience the super–personality of their Creator? They are not reconciled with their Creator. Have you perhaps ignored your Creator up to now, have you never thought about him? Never taken the time to speak to him in your heart? Have we never seriously sought him in reconciliation? One can hardly experience a person by simply ignoring him, not even if this person is our Creator. Or could it be, that we have even denied or hated him, although he has obviously done so much for us? Or have we despised or denied his good commandments? Thou shalt not steal. Thou shalt not commit adultery. Thou shalt not bear false witness. Or let us consider the summary of all God's commandments: "Whatsoever ye would that men should do to you, do ye even so to them: for this *is the law and the prophets" (Matthew 7:12). Today, we hardly can deny that this summary of the law would solve* all political, economical, and also most social problems of our poor world. Yet because we want to be "free" today from God's "infamous" ten commandments, the socialists of the world burden and molest us with innumerable other little parliamentary laws—simply because they want to rid themselves in practice of God's simple ten commandments.

If now God's ten commandments have been disobeyed by us personally, although God entrusted them to us with the best intentions, we will never be able to experience God's personality, for we have thus made ourselves "unacceptable" to him. We have ignored or despised his good commandments and are therefore not reconciled to him, for love of God or of anyone else always includes an initial resolution of enmity, of alienation through reconciliation.

Here we have the basis of all genuine fellowship with the Creator's personality—and with all other personalities. We know God's commandments which serve to govern our relationship to him and to our fellow men. And no doubt we have ignored or disobeyed them. For this reason we have become "unacceptable" and therefore estranged to each other.

How can we find the necessary reconciliation? By asking for forgiveness, if we are serious about this encounter, and this is certainly quite right. If, however, we have done something that needs to be forgiven, who will pay the price of this debt? The price (the fine) for our sin is high. The Bible teaches that the wages of sin (the price for breaking his good laws governing fellowship) is death, i.e. elimination of all mutual fellowship, which equals death.

Chapter 5

He Who Thinks Has To Believe

Is Thought Worthwhile?

Over the centuries, many leading thinkers were also religious. They were, of course, not all Christians, but to a large extent they believed in God, i.e. they were theists. People like Voltaire, Marx, and Lenin, who provide the exception to this rule, have always existed. But the exception proves the rule. Thinkers such as Isaac Newton, Blaise Pascal, and Michael Faraday certainly represent the majority of the thinkers. The great thinker Paul is an eminent example of this conviction. Such men found confirmation of their belief in God, and in some cases of their

Christianity, through their rational thought
and experience.

Many thinkers of today hold the opinion
that Albert Einstein was the greatest scientist of all time. His mathematical, logical
thoughts on the origin and nature of the
universe led him, too, to a firm, logical belief
in the Creator. Above all, his scientific knowledge motivated him to seek to comprehend
the method of creation used by the mysterious
(to him), but rational, Creator — Einstein
came to the conclusion that God did not create
by chance, but rather that he worked according to planned, mathematical, teleonomic,
and therefore — to him — rational guide
lines. For Einstein and others, chance was an
antipode, an antithesis to thought, which he
therefore completely excluded as a means of
creation by a thinking Creator. He attributed
creative, logical thoughts, plans (=
teleonomy) to God and thus decisively re-
jected the modern fashion of attributing all
that exists to chance and therefore to non–
thought, non–teleonomy, and non–logic. The
presumption that a thinking, intelligent creator employed non-thought, i.e. chance, to
create was therefore quite unacceptable to
Einstein, for to accuse any intelligent person
of non-thought in his work, would upset and
insult him enormously.

It is, of course, clear that Einstein did not claim to be a Christian. His convictions in metaphysical matters reached only to a firm belief in a Creator, which motivated Einstein's research in mathematics and physics. Einstein desired to grasp the creative methods employed by God to make the world, for to him the greatest miracle in the universe was that *we can at least in part comprehend it.* We can have our own sensible, logical thoughts about creation. So these conform to the laws of human sense and thought. From this Einstein concluded that the universe (and therefore biology; must have its origin in understanding, thought, concept, mathematics, intelligence, and teleonomy, and not in randomness — chance plus the inanimate laws of nature.

We can say with Einstein that our sense and our thought processes must have something in common with that creative sense and with that creative logic that made the world, for we are capable of at least partly comprehending and following his creative thoughts, even if this capacity is restricted. We are, in principle, capable of thinking "on the creative wavelength" — even if our thoughts will never quite comprehend his thoughts. We slowly begin to have presentiments from afar of the same formative and the same mathematical thought processes as those used by the Creator.

Einstein is, of course, not the only person who has to be mentioned here. Sir James Jeans, the great physicist, Max Planck, the author of the Quantum theory, and Simpson, who discovered the soporific effect of chloroform in surgery ... these were all great thinkers and scientists whose thoughts were influenced by an active belief in the Creator. Simpson was even a diligent evangelical Christian and evangelist. Now, why is it that these men, like many other scientists, were completely convinced believers in God, whereas other thinkers such as Voltaire, Marx, or Lenin came to the opposite conviction regarding a Creator? For some thinkers then, thoughts and science confirmed their theistic beliefs, while for the others the opposite was the case. Is then thought itself worth so little?

Today we still find exactly the same paradox among thinking people. For some people their thoughts seem to confirm their theistic belief, whereas others are led in the opposite direction by their thought processes. Does thought, then, lead astray? Is it in itself unreliable? If thought is an unreliable means of reaching a logical goal, then thought and philosophy should be given up completely!

But then we should cease to be Homo sapiens, for we would thereby give up our very species — the species that thinks! In this case it would be better to live as an apathetic non-thinker, interested only in sensual pleasures such as eating and drinking, than to be an incorrect thinker, enthusing in thought processes which will only lead to the wrong goal anyway. Why can thinkers such as Horkheimer, Habermas, or Marcuse of the School of Frankfurt become decided atheists through their thoughts, while a physicist like Walter Heitler becomes a committed Christian through his thoughts? How is it that eminent scientists such as F.H.C. Crick[1] claim that biology is better understood by physics and chemistry than through the supernatural and metaphysics? Crick is convinced that the scientific thinker would sooner believe in chemistry and physics as the science of life than in metaphysics. Why the "either chemistry or metaphysics" explanation of the origin and meaning of biology? Are these explanations contradictory, or do they supplement each other? Do they really exclude each other,

---

[1] F.H.C. Crick, "Thinking About The Brain," p. 21, *cf* David H. Hubel, "The Brain," *Scientific American*, September, 1979, No. 3, pp.45-52.

as Crick and countless others seemingly assume?

Very many scientists today think just like Crick. They assume that the existence of an understood chemical or physical basis of life — of a known chemical cell metabolism — automatically excludes a metaphysical basis of life: "As soon as we understand cell chemistry, we know that a metaphysical explanation of life becomes superfluous." As this school of thought is taught avidly and dogmatically, indeed almost universally, in most schools and high schools, we must consider it more closely, for many honest thinking scientists are absolutely and unshakeably convinced that the mere existence of proof for a chemical basis of life and of cell metabolism automatically and simultaneously totally excludes any metaphysical basis of life.

Thus a thinker who knows the Krebs cycle or the Embden-Meyerhof pathway and realizes their significance in providing biology with energy, will, according to the above principle of thought, automatically put in question any metaphysical basis of life. According to the modern school of thought, this is the enlightened approach which is far superior to and more intelligent than the ideas of those thinking in metaphysical terms, who still believe in God as a real biological factor. At least many scientists, including myself, were brought up in this manner in our biochemistry laboratory.

A physical-chemical explanation of the basis of life thus supposedly destroys all metaphysical "superstition" within the realm of biology — this is the modern parole. Supposedly "science destroys religion." Is this so?

Crick and many others like him thought that the mere discovery of the fact that man and all biological beings are, materially seen, chemically based machines and mechanisms, simultaneously, authoritatively, and automatically discredited metaphysics as the basis of the origin and nature of man and biology. The assumption is quietly made, of course, that the time-space continuum represents the entire universal reality. It is for this reason, that, from a scientific viewpoint, no metaphysical reality can exist. If it does not exist, then, of course it simply cannot have provided the biological mechanisms for man or for biology. Therefore, once man's chemical and physical basis and the mechanisms involved have been discovered, there is nothing more left to discover about man.

So how did Crick reach the conviction that every newly understood metabolic pathway progressively excludes a metaphysical origin of life? This opinion rules almost the entire thinking scientific world today, although it is obviously irrational.

In order to prevent any misunderstanding, we shall repeat Crick's belief once more: Each newly understood chemical metabolic pathway renders any metaphysical origin of life even more unlikely than it was before this discovery.

What exactly does this conviction express? In reality, just that every new piece of understanding concerning the mode of action of any machine will render more unlikely the creation and conception of this machine by an engineer outside the machine! Thus, the greater our understanding of any machine mechanisms, the less likely it becomes that the machine was designed and built by an engineer outside the machine! *The more we understand how the machine functions, the more certain it becomes that no engineer, but the machine itself (made of matter), built the machine!* In other words, the better we understand the mechanism and functions of a cylinder head, the more certain it becomes that the iron of the cylinder head (or light metal) designed and constructed the head! The better we understand a radio, the more certain does it become that the wires built the apparatus itself!

Crick's statement is obviously slightly irrational! Those scientists who believe similarly must also be irrational! Perhaps the Neanderthalers were right after all in their evaluation of modern man — that he is emotional and not rational. In reality, of course, says Crick, the greater the complexity of the machine and its functions, the more certain it is that non–teleonomic matter built them without design from outside! This constitutes modern logical ability?!

Our Dog

When we were still children on the farm in England, we had a faithful guard, a sheepdog, who loved us children very much. Nothing could ever have happened to us in the dog's presence, for she always looked after us and our parents faithfully. One day when my father was suddenly attacked in the open field by a furious Wessex saddleback sow whose young had temporarily been taken away for veterinary reasons, the dog, at great risk to her own safety, of course, reacted immediately and bit firmly into the raging animal's hock and held on with all her strength until my father and we children could run to safety. I have never forgotten that — the great loy-

alty, intelligence, and immediate understanding of our sheepdog, Folly. The same sort
of thing sometimes happened to us with the
geese, who often became angry, especially
when with their young ones, and then attacked us. The dog always defended us
adroitly.

Folly was a bitch, and once when she had
her own pups, we unwittingly went into her
kennel and took the newly born puppies into
our hands. Normally a bitch would have bit-
ten us immediately, for no one is ever allowed
to touch the puppies. But she only begged us
with her eyes and with whimpers to give her
the puppies back. I can still see her glowing
eyes today. My parents were very angry with
us when they discovered what we had done in
our ignorance.

Now, our dog Folly had one great weakness. She loved to lie on Mother's couch in the
living room, But at certain times of the year
she always shed her coat, which was not
exactly good for the lovely couch. So she was
banned from the couch, which she understood
very well. She then avoided the couch, at least
she did so in Mother's presence. One evening
the entire family was out. Folly was locked
into the kitchen so that she could not be
tempted to misuse Mother's couch. Yet there
was one way by which she could still procure

a pleasant evening on the couch: Folly knew how to open certain doors. A small back staircase connected the kitchen with the hall and the living room via a large main oak staircase. Obviously, the following happened: hardly had we left, when Folly opened a kitchen door, trotted up the back staircase, then down the large front main staircase and then walked through the living room over to the couch, where she made herself wonderfully comfortable.

Now when we came home in the Bentley late that evening, our dog heard us from afar — the exhaust on those cars could hardly be missed! Obviously, she must quickly have trotted up the front staircase and down the back stairs into the kitchen, where she was waiting to greet us, as usual. Normally she was overjoyed at our arrival. But this time she was clearly miserable; she tried to "grin" (she could do that very well indeed), but without success. Her tail was between her legs and she slunk around us all — she wanted to rejoice, for she loved us, but she simply could not.

My father noticed this immediately and asked her what she had done now — one could "talk" to the dog very well. With every word Folly's misery visibly increased and now she even began to whimper. Mother understood quicker than Father. She had stolen nothing.

So she took Folly straight to the couch, which, of course, was covered with hair. My mother scolded her properly and gave her a few hard slaps. Folly then lay down on her back, thus of course exposing all the soft parts of her abdomen. In this manner dogs demonstrate their capitulation. From then on the opponent can do whatever he likes with the one who capitulates thus. The victor, if he is a dog, could, of course, immediately tear out a dog's bowels in this position. Thus this position demonstrates total capitulation.

My father, who understood dogs well, then gave the dog some signs of affection and forgiveness (stroking her and talking to her kindly). She stood up, licked his hands and those of my mother (hands that had punished her) and went humbly, but confidently to her food in the kitchen. Fellowship with the family had been reestablished by capitulation, followed by reconciliation.

Reconciliation and Fellowship

If a Creator does exist (a fact which any non-prejudiced, thinking person must surely admit), who is super-intelligent, omniscient, omnipresent, and super-personal, it is only to be expected that he would be interested in his

creation in the form of people. As both —
Creator and created — are persons, both sides
will be capable of cultivating personal fellowship. However, they will only find such fellowship within the laws governing interpersonal
behavior. If sin (infringement of these laws) of
any sort exists between the two parties, it will
have to be removed by capitulation and reconciliation before fellowship can be really enjoyed.

The above principles provide us with a
reply to the problem of a subjective experience
of God's personality, which some experience
and others do not. *Everyone* can experience
his personality on the basis of capitulation
and reconciliation, for Christ became man
and died to make this reconciliation available
to all people. Naturally, only those people who
recognize their need to be reconciled will experience this reconciliation, for it was not
necessary to die for the self-righteous, to rec-
oncile them!

Christ's forgiveness reestablishes the
interpersonal contact between God and man
through reconciliation. But it is only with
personal reconciliation and forgiveness that
one begins to establish fellowship with God
and to enjoy him. Only then does one begin to
enjoy his beauty, character, and perfection. It
is, perhaps, justified to say that all tensions

and estrangements in Christian and other
circles develop because people do not know
this joy or because they no longer actively
cultivate it. Even in God's material creation
we can feel something of this overflowing
creative joy. The sheer beauty of the tulip, of
Daphnia in March, of lilac in May, and of
asters in autumn all testify to this joy. The
leaping calves and laughing young people
that we see everywhere testify of the same
great joy of the Creator. Even the shadows of
death yield to the glory of the resurrection.

But how can mortal men experience fellowship with such an eternal, joyous, resur-
recting Creator? The difference between him
and us is too great; we cannot establish direct
fellowship with him. Our "wavelength" is too
different from his "wavelength." God lives in
a dimension which is sealed off from our
dimension of time and matter by an event
horizon. The "species difference" between
God and humans is so great that it cannot be
bridged directly. In addition, we are, as sin-
ners, "unacceptable" to God, which would
exclude real fellowship even if we could approach him.

The Godman

When Christ became man he revealed
God's nature and character in human form.
This is a tremendous fact; God, the eternal
Creator, from now on is, "on the same wavelength" as humans. God became a *real biological man,* of the same biological species, just
like we are. To this is added another and even
greater fact: since Christ never gave up his
adopted humanity, a *true man has remained
God.* "Whosoever has seen me [the man] has
seen the Father [God]," said Jesus Christ
(John 14:9). "I and the Father are one" (John
10:30). These words show that Christ is the
second person of the Trinity and that he was
God before he became man and remained God
even as a man.

Now we are in a position to understand a
little better God's person, his ways with us,
his thoughts and his plans, for since the resurrection of Christ, a *man,* Christ, the
Godman is ruling God's throne. The rule of
the heavenly kingdom lies in the hands of a
man, who loves men so much that he died for
them and rose again from the dead. The man
to whom was given all power in heaven and on
earth speaks as we do, thinks as we do, re-
joices as we do, knows the troubles of life and
death as we do, for he died as we do, and rose

from the dead as we all shall. At last, complete
communication, complete fellow-ship between man and God and God and man is
possible. Two types of personalities — man
and Godman — are indeed reconciled.

Thus God's plan for us become plain. He
wants to make renewed beings out of us, so
that we can not only regain our original purpose at creation, but so that we even surpass
it. It will be far more glorious with us than
with Adam in paradise. Christ's character led
to his crucifixion — but with the crucifixion it
led also to the greatest conceivable glorifica-
tion of God. Thus was an entire world saved to
a new kind of life, for men will make Christ's
attitude their goal, resulting in an almost
equally great glory. God's image, but even
better than in the beginning in Adam's paradise, is God's purpose for us. For this reason
we also have to go through the shadow of
death here on earth just like Christ did.[2] But
we must never lose the goal from our sight, for
in both cases the goal is paradise with God
himself, who created us for this eternal purpose.

---

[2] *cf* A. E. Wilder-Smith: *Why Does God Allow It?* TWFT
Publishers, Costa Mesa, Ca. (1990).

Man As God

Any scientifically-thinking person will immediately ask whether God really did historically become man in Christ ... whether the entire story was not an invention of the disciples, later on. We can best resolve these doubts by asking ourselves what we ourselves would expect of a man who in his inner self was and is God, the Creator? If we formulate such a question, we find that the entire biblical report on Christ appears to be genuine on all counts, and also that it is uniform. Seldom does a forged "report" agree in all details like the report on Christ. Just try to present some thought-up story to any experienced judge! The judge will nearly always discover contradictions if the story really is a fake. But Christ's entire historical testimony fits together perfectly. The internal uniformity of the report does ring true. Let us examine the following reports for their veracity:

Before Christ died, he clearly told his disciples and the world that he was going to Jerusalem to die there for the propitiation of all men's sins. However, he added clearly that after three days he would rise again from the dead. What normal mortal man would dare to make two such predictions.

The Pharisees reported this prediction
that he would rise after three days to Pilate,
for the words of Christ were well known everywhere. What would happen to the Pharisees if these prophecies really were fulfilled?
For this reason, the Pharisees requested
guards for the grave, to prevent any theft of
the corpse (Matt. 27:6). The officer on crucifixion duty and who saw Christ die, spontaneously testified that the man who was crucified
was truly the Son of God (Matt. 27:54). Over
five hundred people saw Christ after his crucifixion and his death (I Cor. 15:6). Some of
them talked with him about biblical and other
subjects, and even ate with him. These people
could easily have contradicted the Apostle
Paul's report, for at that time many of them
were still living. No normal person who had
thus been crucified and martyred could have
recovered as well after three days as Christ
did.

Lazarus' resurrection, four days after his
public burial, took place quite openly. Even
Christ's enemies, the Pharisees, could not
deny the truth of this resurrection testimony,
it was much too well known. This even provided an excellent testimony that Christ was
the Son of God, which the Pharisees simply
could not deny. For this reason, they tried to
undo Christ's deed by plotting to kill Lazarus,

for many people believed on the Son of God as
a logical consequence of Lazarus resurrection.

The feeding of the five thousand and of the
four thousand continued in another way the
same testimony to Christ's deity. Either these
testimonies are true, or they are not true. The
evidence for their truth is, however, so strong
that even the Pharisees were prepared to take
to murder to erase it. It was so strong, that
there was such a great gathering of the
people, coming and going continually, so that
Christ did not even have time to eat (Mark
6:31).

Could any different behavior from that of
Christ be expected if God really became man?
If God truly became man, then surely we
would expect him to become a man like Christ
became. Would we expect him to become an
abnormal man like many of our present kings,
ministers, presidents, or dictators? If God as
man had appeared in pomp, then many people
would quite rightly doubt whether God really
did become a real man. The life story of Christ
in the Gospels and also in Isaiah corresponds
with what we would expect of a human being
who really is God, the Highest. One only has
to read carefully through the Gospel of John
to become convinced by the evidence of the
Lord Jesus Christ's superiority in character.

The internal evidence for the truth of John's
testimony shines clearly through every sen-
tence of this unique account.

A Few Conclusions

Two types of evidence or report exist
which give us information about the Creator's
nature: (1) the evidence provided by creation
itself, which is well known to all thinking,
observant people, irrespective of whether or
not they possess the Holy Scriptures. Our
Neanderthalers have shown us what conclusions honest, thinking people can reach, even
though they do not own a Bible. (2) The evidence provided by the Holy Scriptures. In the
Bible, Paul writes much about the revelation
of God. God reveals himself through his Word.
Paul also mentions that the Bible recognizes
evidence of type (1), i.e. the witness of nature
(Romans 1).

Man may use both types of evidence, that
of nature and of revelation, to reach firm
conclusions about the nature of God and the
purpose of human existence. But can he rely
on his thought processes in these considera-
tions? Is his brain a reliable instrument in
this search for God and for the meaning behind human existence? The answer is, alas —

as so often — both yes and no! Paul the
Apostle often challenges us to reflect, i.e. to
think. He demanded concentrated attention
from his audience, i.e. careful thought when
he spoke of the Messiah (Acts 28:26, 27). Thus
he reckons that the thought processes must
be intrinsically reliable. On the other hand
the same Apostle warned specifically against
the unreliability of certain types of human
thought: "But the natural man receiveth not
the things of the Spirit of God: for they are
foolishness unto him: *neither can he know
them* because they are spiritually discerned"
(I Cor, 2:14).

So here we have an apparently paradoxi-
cal situation. On the one hand, Paul admon-
ishes men and challenges them to think sensibly with him. Thus, he behaves as if men
really can safely think. On the other hand he
firmly states that certain people *cannot recognize* certain things, i.e., *they cannot think
them out.* In the areas in which they cannot
think, they no longer possess any capacity to
comprehend, they cannot understand. What
is the solution to this contradiction?

As so often is the case with problems such
as these, deeper knowledge lies under the
surface of the difficulties. In several places in
the Bible, Paul teaches that human knowledge, human capacity for thought and human

receptive ability are not *static*, but *dynamic*
factors. In principle, most people are capable
of thinking problems through, aided by their
ratio, until they reach a conclusion. This capacity is like computer capacity and depends
on the brain's wiring.

If, however, a person with his thinking
apparatus comes to a *conclusion* which requires *action*, then he has two alternatives.
Either he can obey the intelligent decision
which he reached by valid thought processes,
or he can *refuse to obey it*, for an intellectual
decision does not, of course, *of itself* alter or
determine a person's *way of life*. What a person *does* with the intellectual decision, how he
handles it and *acts upon it*, that is quite a
different matter. The two processes together,
the thinking and the obeying of thought decisions, these intellectual decisions and actions
condition a person's *conscience* and therefore
character. The conscience needs intellectual
enlightenment by the thought processes. But
if a person *obeys* the demands of his conscience which has been enlightened by intelligent thought, he becomes filled with joy *and*
his thought processes can further enlighten
his conscience regarding other problems. If,
however, he does *not* obey the demands of his
conscience, then (1) his conscience is injured,
scarred, and hardened. Thus the basis of his

inner "voice" will be lost. But a second process occurs simultaneously with the hardening of his conscience; (2) the reasoning processes, the *ratio*, the thought processes which led to the enlightenment of his conscience, become darkened. The person suffering from a hardened conscience will no more be able to *discern*. He will be able to develop *less ratio* in that area. His *thought processes* become dulled, together with his *conscience*. Thus conscience and the thought processes which condition knowledge (and conscience) are dynamic and not static factors.

It is important to realize that not only the Bible teaches this dynamic view of the thought processes and of the conscience. Our daily experience in life has taught us just the same, for if a criminal commits his first murder, his conscience and also his ratio (reasoning power) suffer extensively. But after he has killed another twenty victims, his conscience is hardened. Many such people even then begin to "justify" their murders with their thought processes! The murders serve "the cause of freedom," "of revolution," or even of "human good!" In their inner selves they know very well that violence and murder solve no problems. But in order to silence the accusations of their conscience, they begin to "rationalize" and to justify their misdeeds.

Thus their conscience becomes dulled *and* their capacity for cool and rational thought slowly or quickly is lost.

The human *capacity for conviction and thought persuasion* thus depends on a delicate sensitive mechanism, which can easily be damaged by misuse. Examples of such abuse are not difficult to find. Under Hitler certain SS men killed their prisoners "like flies." They had ditches dug, then lined up the prisoners, who had dug the ditches, in front of the holes. Thereupon they mowed the prisoners down with machine guns so that they buried themselves. Some commanders enjoyed this spectacle so much that they even had it accompanied by orchestras of prisoners playing Wagner's music! The pleasure obtained by the commanders from these proceedings grew with practice. At first they found these murders revolting. With time they eventually dulled their conscience by misuse and the terror of their deeds caused them less trouble. Finally they enjoyed their "rationalized" misdeeds. These horrors were even *rationalized* under the heading of "loyalty to the Fatherland." The functions of the ratio (mind) and the conscience are not static, but dynamic!

When a young biology student hears for the first time from his professor that life and the entire cell originate from stochastic chemical reactions and not from any extra-material planning or concept, he is usually intellectually shocked and even horrified. He thinks of the structure of the eye, the liver, the bee orchid, or of a virus. His ratio (mind) rebels against being taught that structure, concepts, machines, language, code, information, and projects originate from stochastic (random) phenomena. He knows that this contradicts experimental experience. Never did any *machine* develop spontaneously from any inorganic matter. He comes to this conclusion simply because so much speaks for the *planning* of all biological and other machines by a creator. This thought process now registers with his conscience. He must therefore *act* and own up to the fact that he cannot and indeed will not believe this biological chance, Darwinian nonsense.

Yet, at the same time he knows that he must pass his exams. His professor is likely to fail him if there is any suspicion that he does not conform to evolutionary theory. So the student under pressure denies the insight of his thought processes and rational mind, thus injuring his conscience. He joins in the chorus with everyone else, intoning that stochastic

phenomena created the super—machine we
call the biological cell. Thus he claims that the
greatest reduction of entropy and indeed the
most sublime order or machine ever seen by
the world, namely man and the human brain,
developed with no plan and with no concept of
any sort. By this means he denies not only his
own rationality and common sense, but at the
same time his Creator too, by willingly believing nonsense. In this manner the mass "hysteria" we mentioned previously develops. Finally he is no longer able to recognize the fact
that this position represents an unconscio-
nable misuse of the function of the thought
processes lent him by his Creator for use and
not for abuse. Conscience and the ability to
reason have thus both been injured by doing
despite to reason in the interest of conformity
and personal advancement.

Soon it becomes impossible to converse
with him seriously on the subject without
causing anger. He can no longer talk in an
unprejudiced manner in this whole area of
thought ... without emotions being unpleas-
antly aroused. Those who disagree with him
and do insist on reasoning will be eliminated
by denigration. Soon he may ask with Pilate:
"What is truth?" (John 18:38), even though
the truth is looking right into his brain. By
lack of courage or weakness of the will there

was insufficient determination to follow the
demands of plain rational thought processes,
insight, and common sense which results in
damaging both the conscience and the
thought processes. Even the Apostle Paul said
that men were *"without [rational] excuse"* if
they denied the testimony of their Creator in
the testimony of all nature (Rom. 1). Func-
tional damage of this type both in the conscience and in the thought processes is surely
manifest in many of the symptoms shown by
modern society. How much of this may be due
to evolutionary teaching in modern schools
and universities?

Let us risk summarizing some of these
thoughts with a simple allegory. The human
brain can be compared with a coffee mill.
Given good coffee beans, it produces good,
refreshing, stimulating coffee. But if small
round pebbles, instead of coffee beans, are fed
into the mill, the mill will be damaged and at
the same time produce no coffee at all. The
human brain is the coffee mill, which gladly
grinds facts, theses, dissertations, and ideas
like coffee beans. The "coffee" (conclusions,
understanding, theses) thus produced re-
freshes us. If, however, a man feeds his "coffee
mill" (brain) with impossible "facts," theses,
dissertations, and ideas, with "artifacts" (i.e.,
with "stones") and pseudoscience, the brain

(his "coffee mill") will be functionally damaged — and that man does not receive the
"coffee" (understanding) that he requires ...
he is deprived of coherent, sensible theses on
the meaning of life and the purpose of our
human existence, becoming thereby frustrated.

In order to regain our lost purpose in life
and to dispel the modern frustrations of
"meaningless" life, we urgently need the courage of our convictions to obey the religious,
scientific, and philosophical conclusions
reached by our reasonable thought. A Creator
does exist! We must openly stand by this fact.
And this Creator purchased our redemption
and reconciliation with himself through
Christ's death and resurrection. If we openly
stand by this fact, our conscience and also our
understanding will both flourish. As a result
we will experience him in our hearts in the
Christian rebirth. Thus the long-yearned-for
fellowship between man and his God will be
reestab-lished, and thus do we begin to regain
by stages Paradise lost.

The Natural Sciences Know Nothing of Evolution
Uses the Natural Sciences themselves to show the error of evolu-tionary theory. $6.99

AIDS: Fact without Fiction
A comprehensive, up-to-date pre-sentation of the facts about this new plague. Discusses its discovery, its spreading about the world, its medical effects and the efforts to over-come the disease as well as the politics involved. $7.99

The Scientific Alternative to Neo-Darwinian Evolutionary Theory
Dr. Wilder-Smith's latest scientific exposé of evolutionary theory. Presents an alternative. Introduces the "I" factor for which evolutionists have no answer. $6.99

The Day Nazi Germany Died
An autobiography by Beate Wilder-Smith, Dr. Wilder-Smith's wife. An eyewitness account of life in Nazi Germany and the Russian and Allied invasion. $4.99

**The Author
Dr. A.E. Wilder-Smith**